What Peop
Seven S.
Religion Classes

"This is a remarkable tool for all catechists. Gwen and Joe are clearly practitioners who know the realities, the potential, and the challenges of the catechist. In an immanently readable style, interspersed with their own stories of both success and failure, the authors offer practical ways to make the most out of each catechetical session for catechized and catechist alike!"

Carole M. Eipers, D.Min.
Director, Office for Religous Education
Archdiocese of Chicago

"*Seven Steps to Great Religion Classes* can remind one that precious things come in small packages. This small handbook promises to be a precious gift to countless catechists striving to be more effective teachers in our faith communities today with their demanding challenges."

Carol Frances Jegen, BVM
Senior Professor of Pastoral Studies
Loyola University Chicago

"This book is an easy-to-follow road map for the volunteer catechist. In simple, direct language, Joe and Gwen discuss the essentials of good catechesis: how to plan a lesson, how to create the right atmosphere, how to engage the minds and hearts of the children, how to ask real questions, how to help the children pray, how to handle discipline problems. These are the things every pastor and DRE wants the parish catechists to know 'by heart'."

Kieran Sawyer, SSND
Director of the Tyme Out Youth Center
Stone Bank, WI

"*Seven Steps to Great Religion Classes* is a book that inspires. Oh sure, it informs too: every chapter is chock full of helpful hints and sage advice for teaching religion to today's young. But more importantly, the book inspires: every chapter includes reflective questions, an original prayer, and space for personal journalling."

Melannie Svoboda, SND
Author, *Teaching is Like...Peeling Back Eggshells,
Jesus I'm A Teacher Too: Guidance and Inspiration from the Gospel*

"*Seven Steps to Great Religion Classes* is an excellent resource for new catechists and a superb checklist for the not-so-new teacher. It provides a succinct yet well developed presentation of each topic, with practical examples and user-friendly information."

Karen Leslie
Author, *Faith and Little Children: A Guide for Parents and Teachers*
Media Resource Coordinator, Diocese of Erie, PA

"Just walk these steps with Gwen Costello and Joseph Paprocki and you're on the right road to success as a catechist. Their book contains everything you need to know before stepping into the classroom. What a gold mine of practical ideas!

Gail Thomas McKenna
Author, *Through the Year with the DRE* and
Models and Trends in Religious Education

"Whatever your level of catechetical expertise, you'll find in *Seven Steps to Great Religion Classes* the how-to information you need for effective ministry. You'll also find lots of inspiration and ideas. Gwen Costello and Joseph Paprocki share with the reader the basic skills for your absolutely important ministry of catechetics."

Dr. Greg Dues
Author, *Teaching Religion with Confidence and Joy*

GWEN COSTELLO

JOE PAPROCKI

Seven Steps to **Great** Religion Classes

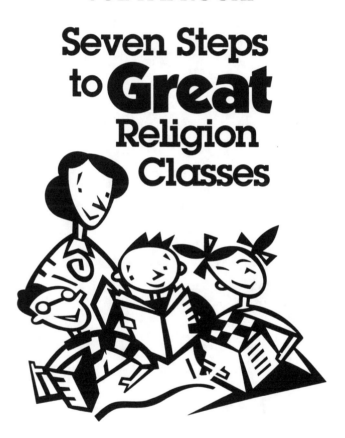

TWENTY-THIRD PUBLICATIONS

Mystic, CT 06355

Twenty-Third Publications
185 Willow Street
P.O. Box 180
Mystic, CT 06355
(860) 536-2611
(800) 321-0411

ISBN 0-89622-934-3
Library of Congress Catalog Card Number 98-60622
Printed in the U.S.A.

Contents

Seven Steps to Great Religion Classes

Introduction

S o you are a catechist! This can be good news for you or bad news, depending on your perspective. It's good news if you love children, if you enjoy sharing your faith, and if you have patience and understanding. It's bad news if you lack all of the above. No book or video or course can make being a catechist good news for those who do it grudgingly. But such resources, including this book, can make teaching religion easier and sometimes even a joy when you generously give yourself to it.

If you are this kind of volunteer, you can expect to learn here about skills that will help you to more effectively proclaim the content of your lessons. In chapter one, "Meeting the Challenge," we will look at qualities and skills that an "ideal" catechist would most likely possess.

In chapter two, "Planning the Best Lessons," we will examine the process of lesson planning, from setting goals and objectives, to employing a variety of methods for implementing the lesson, including lecture, discussion, questions and answers, small group work, role-playing, and a variety of other creative methods.

In chapter three, "Creating the Right Environment," we will take a look at the basic skills catechists need to create a positive environment, from the moment of stepping into a class to the end of the lesson.

In chapter four, "Ways to Motivate and Involve Children," we will look at strategies for leading discussions that focus on the students sharing and the catechists facilitating. We'll look at some simple skills for asking questions so that you don't end up answering every question yourself.

In chapter five, "Handling Discipline Problems," we will talk about one of the most challenging areas of your teaching. We will look at prevention techniques most of all, but also at skills and techniques for handling problems if and when they arise. Our goal will be to help you maintain a positive environment and an attitude of mutual respect.

In chapter six, "Helping Children to Pray," we will look at various types of prayer experiences that you can share with your class. We will offer information about "setting" as well as skills and techniques for leading various types of prayer experiences.

In our final chapter, "Evaluating Yourself," we will review what we have learned and talk about ways to evaluate how well you have incorporated your new skills and teaching techniques.

Also included with each chapter are questions for personal reflection to be pondered before you read the chapter and questions for reflection and/or discussion at the end of the chapter. These questions can be used privately, but they will also be useful for guiding discussions with your DRE and other catechists.

Finally, at the end of each chapter you will find a prayer that expresses the concerns, hopes, fears, and dreams of a catechist. We invite you to reflect on these prayers and then write out your responses to them in the space provided. Our hope is that you will eventually want to spend time every day prayerfully reflecting on your very special call to be a catechist.

May this call be for you very good news indeed.

Chapter One

Meeting the Challenge

Before you start reading, think about these questions: Which qualities and skills in your opinion would an ideal catechist most likely have? And what about you, which do you have? Which qualities do you still need?

*A*re you one of those people who loves working with children, especially in areas of faith development? Or are you someone who got into teaching because a DRE or pastor asked you to? Or, maybe you're somewhere in between. You like the idea of teaching religion, but you're not sure you know how. Believe it or not, people become catechists for all kinds of reasons. Some really love sharing their faith with children and feel called by the Holy Spirit to proclaim their faith. Others feel that children need adult role models, adults who can share the Word of God with them and help them grow as Christians. Still others want to serve the parish in some way and are invited by parish leaders to try teaching religion. And then there's you.

Whatever *your* reason, serving as a catechist is a wonderful privilege. But to be honest, we know that it is also very challenging. If you are preparing to become a catechist for the first time, no doubt you have concerns about beginning your ministry. If you have served as a catechist before, you know that this ministry has its ups and downs. But whether you are a beginner or a veteran, there is always room for improvement in the area of teaching skills. That's what we will be focusing on in this book.

You Are People of Faith

We would like to say at the outset that we have great admiration for you as catechists. Without a doubt you are people with great dedication, enthusiasm, knowledge of the faith, and deep spirituality. You love children, and you want to proclaim the Word of God to them. At the same time, you realize that to teach about Scripture and the tradition of the church requires a certain level of confidence in classroom management and teaching skills.

How to prepare a lesson, how to use a variety of creative approaches, how to engage children and keep them on task, how to create a faith environment, how to lead discussions, how to ask questions, how to handle discipline, how to lead prayer experiences: these are the skills that allow you to unleash the power of God's Word, but they need to be fine-tuned.

In this book we are going to cover the nuts and bolts of these skills within a faith context. Whether you are teaching at home, or in a traditional setting with children in rows of desks, or sitting on the floor in a circle around a candle, you will need these basic skills to be a successful catechist.

Who Is the Ideal Catechist?

While it's true that we don't live in an ideal world, it is important for us to strive for ideals. Let's imagine for a moment that we are looking for the ideal catechist, someone who is very successful at his or her ministry. What qualities would that person possess?

We consider the following to be among the most important (though not necessarily in this order): active in the church community, commitment, enthusiasm, flexibility, knowledge of Scripture and tradition, love of children, patience, prayerfulness, punctuality, self-assurance, a sense of humor, and willingness to be a team player. This list will seem a bit overwhelming at first glance, but you probably already possess many, if not most, of these qualities to some degree or another. Let's look at a few of them closely and you'll see what we mean.

The fact that you are a catechist or preparing to be one says that you are already *active in your church community,* and obviously you are *committed* to serving your parish as a catechist, at least for this year.

In many ways, *enthusiasm* and *a sense of humor* go together. If you can laugh at your own mistakes, not take yourself too seriously, and if you can relax enough to enjoy those you teach, you will be enthusiastic and look forward to the time you spend together. *Love of children* naturally follows here. If you love them, you will enjoy them and appreciate their efforts to grow in faith and to respond to what you are teaching.

Patience and *flexibility* are two other qualities that go hand in hand. If you are patient, you will be flexible. You won't get upset if a lesson moves in a direction you hadn't planned. When you are flexible, you will be able to move back to where you wanted to be without getting angry or impatient with the class.

While we don't have space here to comment on all the qualities of an ideal catechist, we would like to focus on one more, prayer. *Prayerfulness* is an essential quality for a catechist because without it there can be no relationship with God, the one whose message we proclaim. Prayerfulness assumes that we believe in God's presence within us, that we believe God is within each child we teach, and that we depend on God for guidance and inspiration.

All of these qualities make it possible for us to share our faith, and we should all make a regular practice of taking a quick inventory before and after we teach to reflect on these qualities, asking ourselves to what extent they are manifested in our ministry. Which ones do we need to improve upon? Which ones are missing that would make a difference in our approach?

Or, you might want to focus on one quality in particular. For example, if you want to focus on prayerfulness, make a conscious effort to add three or four prayerful moments to your lesson. After the lesson, analyze and evaluate how well you did this. It is important not to expect too much of ourselves all at once, so focusing on one characteristic at a time works best for many catechists.

Skills and Techniques

Let's take a look now at some of the skills and techniques we might expect an ideal catechist to possess. On this list we might include planning good lessons, leading prayer experiences, communicating effectively, involving children, handling discipline, using a variety of teaching methods, asking questions properly, leading discussions well, offering children positive feedback, and working well with the text.

An experienced catechist will have had to work fairly hard to develop any or all of these skills. Being a catechist doesn't come naturally to most of us. We may love children but may have to work at polishing the skills that make us confident proclaimers. Desire to be a good catechist is not enough. This is especially true when it comes to the first skill we mentioned, lesson planning.

A catechist can't just walk into a room full of children and proceed to talk about God's love with no particular pattern or plan. Teaching a good lesson is more complex than that. Good lesson planning requires familiarity with the content: what is the lesson all about; what is at the heart of it? What would you most want children to remember from it? A good catechist will always read the material in the text beforehand to answer these questions. The teacher's manual will suggest numerous ways to proceed, but you are the one who will have to choose the methods and activities that will work best for you and your particular group of children. (Note: we will cover lesson planning in more detail in chapter two.)

A Common Challenge

We can almost guarantee that if a catechist *does not prepare well,* does not know the lesson well, there will be discipline problems. And that brings us to another characteristic on our list. Discipline is one of the greatest challenges for most catechists. It can be very discouraging when children are talking to one another, giggling, or throwing paper airplanes around the room instead of paying attention to your lesson.

Remember, however, that discipline is a by-product of good teaching, and if you have planned your lesson well, children won't have time to be disruptive. Yet, there will always be *some* degree of discipline problems no matter how experienced a catechist is or how well planned a lesson is. That's why later in this book (in chapter five) we will look at maintaining discipline in much more detail.

Again while all of the skills and techniques we have listed are valuable, leading prayer experiences is among the most important. Leading prayer is a different skill from managing a classroom, and if you are coming from a background where you were rarely encouraged to pray with others, you will find this even more challenging.

Prayer is a very personal experience, but if we as adults feel uncomfortable, just imagine how children feel when we invite them to pray! It takes a great deal of skill to put everyone at ease and to make prayer experiences comfortable. That's why it is important to involve children in such experiences slowly, step by step. Little by little they will begin to feel comfortable praying spontaneously, meditating, writing out prayer petitions, serving as readers, and so on. Again we will say much more about leading prayer experiences later in this book (in chapter six).

We Are Not Born Teachers

It's true that some people are natural teachers, born to it, as it were, but most of us are not. The basic skills of teaching and classroom management, however, can be acquired by anyone who possesses the confidence to serve as a catechist and the determination to practice the needed skills.

We will try to show in this series how dedicated and confident catechists can improve their ministry by acquiring and exploring these skills. Remember, we already have the most powerful teaching material at our fingertips, the Word of God. We don't have to make our faith exciting, it already is. We just have to facilitate the proceedings properly so that God's power can come through us with those we teach.

We ask you above all to remember that learning to teach

better and better is an experience that takes time, patience, trial and error, and deep faith. You will sometimes have wonderful lessons, sometimes not so wonderful. You will sometimes perfectly communicate what you want to say and at other times not so perfectly. You will sometimes have very spiritual experiences and sometimes ones that do not touch hearts. But from all of this you can grow and learn. And then little by little, before you know it, you will be teaching better and better. That is our hope as we make this journey together.

For Your Reflection and Discussion

•What do you consider your greatest challenge as a catechist? How would you describe this to a co-catechist or your DRE?

•What qualities of the "ideal catechist" do you feel that you already possess? How might you best utilize these qualities in the next class you teach?

•What qualities do you need to improve on? How can you tell? How might you begin to acquire them?

•What skills and techniques of the "ideal catechist" do you feel you possess? In what ways might you use these skills more effectively?

•What skills and techniques do you need to improve on? How can you do this?

•Is there someone in your parish program with whom you would feel comfortable discussing your skills and techniques, a veteran catechist or your DRE, for example?

A Catechist's Prayer

Jesus, Beloved Savior, you have called me to proclaim your Word, and though I feel inadequate for this task, I will rely on you to guide me. Help me to face the challenges teaching brings, to accept my limitations, and to build on my strengths. May I always be an "ideal catechist" in your eyes. Amen.

In My Own Words...

_____

_____

_____

_____

_____

_____

_____

_____

_____

_____

Chapter Two

Planning the Best Lessons

Before you start reading, think about these questions: Do you always do everything you can to be prepared for your classes? Do you use a variety of techniques and activities? Do the children seem interested and involved?

Lesson planning can be a daunting prospect, even for experienced catechists, but it is nevertheless an essential element of a good religion lesson. Consider it something like taking a trip. Would you do it without advance planning? Most of us wouldn't. You need to plan ahead and pick convenient dates. You have to work out an itinerary and make reservations. You have to study tour guides and decide which attractions you will visit. Most of all, you need to pack your bags and take enough money. Few of us would begin a family vacation without making these kinds of preparations. The same is true of our catechetical ministry. Every time you teach a religion lesson, you are setting out on a journey with members of your faith family. The key to making it as fulfilling as possible is planning.

A Solid Foundation

Jesus talked about preparedness in the parable of the house built on rock, and we have come to realize that lesson planning is indeed the solid foundation, the rock on which our teaching ministry is built. We are convinced that if a catechist plans well and is well-prepared, the very core of the teaching process has been achieved.

We have seen some very gifted, enthusiastic, and dedicated people fall flat in the classroom because they weren't prepared to carry out a full lesson. On the other hand, we have seen catechists of average capabilities pull off some of the best classes because they planned ahead and knew exactly what they wanted to accomplish. Planning just makes good sense.

And yet it is not something that comes naturally to everyone. By nature, most of us like to proceed without reading the directions! In catechesis, taking the time to go over the plan and the instructions step by step is a skill that needs to be taught and reinforced, and that's where DREs and Coordinators come in. They usually don't just hand out textbooks and say, "Here. Teach!" They have to provide catechists with the skills of lesson planning just as a coach would provide a marathon runner with a regimen for training.

If your parish doesn't have a DRE or Coordinator, your next best recourse is the teacher's manual that comes with your textbook. The people who write these manuals are often experienced DREs who know a great deal about volunteer catechists like you and the task that lies before you. And, of course, here in this chapter we will address many of the issues involved in lesson planning.

Before getting into specific skills and techniques, however, it's important to say at the outset that before we do any planning, we have to open ourselves to the guidance of the Holy Spirit. When we sit down to prepare, we should always spend a few minutes asking God to open our minds and hearts and to guide our planning.

Think of the children in your class and remind yourself that you are doing God's work, not your own. Beginning with prayer is a crucial step in lesson planning because it places the whole process in the proper context.

Getting Started

So let's assume that you have your textbook or other curriculum materials, you have prayed for guidance, and you have pictured the children in your class. What's next? For us, "what's next" is setting a goal, knowing precisely what we hope to accomplish.

Let's look at the example of a vacation again. Your goal can be compared to your destination. Let's say you plan to go to Hawaii. That's a very broad destination. You need to narrow it down to a more specific one and have a purpose for selecting that location. So, instead of just saying, I'm going to Hawaii," you might continue by saying, "I'm going to visit my aunt and uncle in Honolulu and surprise them for their 50th wedding anniversary." Now that's getting specific. You know your trip will be successful if you actually make it to Honolulu and surprise your aunt and uncle!

The same is true of our lesson planning. A goal is important, but we need to be specific; we need to establish learning outcomes. These are also referred to in your manual as "objectives," statements that clearly articulate the specific expectations and outcomes of the lesson.

Children are more likely to learn when they (and their

teachers), understand what they are expected to learn. Learning outcomes give children and teachers specific goals to pursue, and when they know their exact destination, it's easier to decide on the route to get there.

A learning outcome should specify the content or concept the children will learn or master and the behavior that will indicate successful completion of the lesson. For example, if we use a learning outcome like, "the children will better appreciate the New Testament," it is too broad and vague. How will we ever know if we've succeeded? However, if we say our learning outcome is, "the children will identify the four gospels of the New Testament," we have a precise statement that specifies what is to be learned and tells teachers how they will know if the learning outcome has been achieved.

Focus on the Children

All of us are tempted from time to time to state our goals and learning outcomes as something we are supposed to do. The focus of goals and learning outcomes, however, must be on what the children are going to do. If we have clear, precise, student-focused learning outcomes, the spotlight is shifted away from ourselves and on to the children where it belongs.

Once you have established what the children are to learn, what do you do next? We suggest looking carefully at your teacher's manual (or other curriculum materials) because it will spell out for you the possible ways you can achieve your goal. Most manuals offer a variety of ways to achieve learning outcomes—like the following: reading the text, writing, video viewing, prayer, panel discussions, lectures, games, posters, drawing, music, dialogue (Q&A), guest speakers, projects, group discussions, role-playing, journaling, field trips, storytelling, craft projects, show and tell, and contests. With a list like this, how do you know what to choose? First of all, never select an activity for busy work. If it does not help achieve a learning outcome, don't use it. If your learning outcome is to have children articulate their image of Jesus, then showing them a video or having a guest speaker won't do. If you want children to articulate *their* image of Jesus, they need to express this themselves by journaling, drawing, discussions, role-playing, etc.

Another thing we have learned over the years is that no matter what activity you select, you have to give children very clear directions. Role-playing is a great idea, but be prepared to give clear directions on what is expected and why you are doing the role-plays. The same is true of journaling, crafts, projects, storytelling, etc. In other words, you have to be prepared ahead of time to explain clearly to children what the learning outcome is and how it can be achieved.

The Heart of the Matter

Now, let's look at one more very important part of lesson planning, what we call the heart of the matter. Thomas Groome, who wrote the landmark book, *Christian Religious Education,* offers the following image to help us understand how to approach catechesis.

Imagine that you have a child playing outside, and suddenly the child comes in crying, "Mommy, Mommy." Your first question will be, "What happened? Tell me what happened."

After the child explains that a friend pushed her down, your next question would be, "Why did she do it?" After the child explains that she called her friend a name and stuck out her tongue, you might ask her if she understands why the friend got upset and pushed her. You might also tell her a story of a similar experience from your own life, the classic, "When I was your age...." Finally, you would ask your child what she learned from the experience, bandage her up, and send her on her way.

This story gives us a model for catechesis that Groome calls the "shared praxis approach." In their book, *Creative Catechist,* Janaan Manternach and Carl Pfeifer suggest that there are three lesson-planning movements that correlate with Groome's approach. The first movement is where we *Explore Life* ("Tell me what happened and why..."). The second movement is where we *Share Tradition* ("When I was your age..." or "Let me tell you a story..."). The third movement of our lesson is where we attempt to *Integrate Life and Tradition* ("What did you learn from this experience/my story...?" or "So, how will you be different next time...?").

Keeping these three movements in mind can greatly benefit our lesson planning. They tell us to begin our lesson by focusing on experiences the children are having, and then relate those experiences to our Catholic tradition. Finally, we have to show children how to apply our tradition to their daily living and decisions. Let's look at how this might work if the lesson is about the commandments.

Teaching the Commandments

You might begin by having children name and list some of the rules they live by at home and in school. After discussing the reasons for these rules, share the Exodus story and how God gave Moses the Ten Commandments. You might then read the Scripture story and role-play it. Then comes what we call the "so what?" part of the lesson. You have looked at rules in the children's lives and looked at the story of the Ten Commandments. So what? What will this mean for the children you are teaching in the days and years ahead? How does it apply to them? How will it strengthen their relationship with God? If you have prepared well, you will be able to suggest some practical ways children can apply God's commandments on a daily basis.

The bottom line is, "What difference does this topic make in their spiritual and daily lives and how can we help it make a difference?" Here's where your activities come in. Which approach seems right for your lesson and for your unique group of children? This is the key question for your planning. Once you have answered it, you need to estimate your time and prepare the materials you'll need for your lesson. A good way to do this, by the way, is through mental imagery. Close your eyes and imagine going through the lesson. Visualize all of the things you'll need. Imagine any of the obstacles that might arise. And realistically estimate how long each segment will take with an eye toward "over-planning." In other words, always plan a bit more than you need.

One final note: Always finish your planning where it started...in prayer. Just as you asked the Holy Spirit to guide your planning, thank the Spirit for the inspiration you have received and pray for guidance as you teach your lesson.

Keep in Mind...
Children remember:
20% of what the hear;
30% of what they see;
50% of what they hear and see;
70% of what they say; and
90% of what they do.

Unfortunately, it's a fact that we teachers do 70% of the talking in class and ask 94% of all questions! As we look at the variety of activities available to us, we need to be creative but not gimmicky. Our goal is not to be flashy. Instead, we need to select the activities that will best engage the children and help them achieve the learning outcomes we've identified. In a word, we have to invite a lot more "doing and saying" on the part of the children.

For Your Reflection and Discussion

•What kind of planning do you do before taking a vacation? How much time does it take?

•How much time and preparation do you put into lesson plans? How much time should you put in?

•Do you understand what is meant by goals and learning outcomes? (Identify and offer some examples of these for your next lesson.)

•In your experience, what kinds of problems can planning and preparing overcome or avoid?

•For a typical lesson, what are some of the things that you need to prepare for in advance? How has this benefitted your class?

•Do the children in your class usually leave with a clear notion of how to apply your lesson to their daily living? If not, how might you begin to focus on this?

•What activities (or responses to your lesson) have you found most effective with children? Do these activities help children to make connections between religion and daily life? How can you tell?

A Catechist's Prayer

Jesus, my Savior and Guide, be with me as I plan each lesson this year. Even when I'm tired or discouraged, help me to plan with energy and enthusiasm. Send your Holy Spirit to inspire and encourage me so that in every lesson I may lead your "little ones" closer to you. Amen.

In My Own Words...

_____

_____

_____

_____

_____

_____

_____

_____

_____

_____

_____

_____

Chapter Three

Creating the Right Environment

Before you start reading, think about these questions: Is your teaching space conducive to learning and prayer? What can you do to make it better? What can your parish leaders do to help you create the kind of learning environment you need?

*T*n our previous two chapters, we gave you a general overview of teaching skills and looked more specifically at the skill of lesson planning. We've seen that the key to effective catechesis is a solid lesson plan with clear aims, well-defined learning outcomes, and appropriate activities to help achieve those objectives.

But now we'll examine an important aspect of teaching that is often overlooked: the learning environment. We call this the skill of "setting the stage." Too often, we prepare excellent lessons only to find that the room or setting for our lesson is not conducive to learning, sharing, and praying.

Surroundings Do Matter

Does it really matter where you teach? Didn't Jesus teach wherever a crowd gathered? No, Jesus selected his surroundings very carefully to achieve the greatest impact on his audience. He could have delivered the beatitudes from an easy chair in front of the carpenter shop, but Matthew tells us quite clearly that he went up on the mountainside to deliver his teaching. If we are to teach as Jesus did, we, too, need to pay attention to our surroundings.

Setting the stage for catechesis means stepping out of our lesson planning space and into what might be called an ideal teaching space (at least in imagination).

Before doing this together, we should say clearly that we don't think catechesis should ordinarily be based on a school model. Yet, the majority of catechists do teach in a classroom because that's the only space available in many parishes. However, there is a lot you can do to make a classroom warm and inviting. So, whether your setting is a room in your home, a classroom, a church basement, a room in the convent or rectory, or a fully furnished religion resource room, the bottom line is, you need to pay attention to the details of your surroundings. Let's imagine together then, the ideal setting.

When Children Come In

First of all, when children enter a room, you should be right there greeting them. By their arrival time, you should be ready for them and not doing last-minute lesson preparation. Any room used for religion class should be a welcoming environment, a positive faith environment, and the attitude of the catechist is the most important aspect of welcoming.

Think about it. If you're getting ready for company in your house, you pay attention to many little details that say, "I was expecting you, and you are really welcome." The same is true of our learning environment. We want to communicate to children that we are prepared, we are enthusiastic, and we welcome their arrival.

Another important factor is the seating arrangement. One time I (Joe) walked into a catechist's room and found her sitting with six children at one table while two children each sat at their own separate tables. Thinking that perhaps these two children were discipline problems, I later asked the catechist why she isolated them. She looked puzzled and said, "That's just where they sat." I couldn't help but think that those two children left feeling ignored and unappreciated. Or they chose to isolate themselves and the catechist failed to welcome them into the total group. Seating arrangements can be very important.

When Jesus fed the crowd of 5,000 people, he clearly instructed his disciples to make them sit down on the grass in groups of hundreds and fifties. Out of the chaos of a huge crowd, Jesus created community. Your seating arrangement, too, needs to create a sense of community. Desks that are lined up in straight rows facing the teacher's desk clearly point all the attention to the teacher.

However, having children sit in a circle or semi-circle around a Bible and candle, focuses attention on the Word of God and on the children. This is especially important because you will often be incorporating prayer into your class experiences. Also, you need your seating arrangement to be flexible for the variety of activities you plan to include.

If you're using a borrowed classroom, be sure to respect the arrangement you found when you entered. Enlist the help of some of the children or an aide to move the furniture back where it belongs. Moving things around is a lot of work, but it's truly worth the effort.

A Space for Prayer

One summer I (Joe) was rearranging furniture in our parish classrooms and I moved a small table out of our preschool room to make more space for the children to play. When I proudly showed my handiwork to the catechist, she said sadly, "But you took away my prayer table."

Not knowing what she was referring to, I denied all charges. She then explained to me that she always placed a Bible, a candle, and a bowl of holy water on that small table, and she gathered the children around it to bless themselves with the water and listen to a Bible story before their lesson. Needless to say, I returned the table.

Whether you call it a prayer station or just a table with a Bible, it is important to create a "sacred space" in your class, preferably in the center where it can be the focus of attention. By placing a Bible in your midst, you are communicating a powerful message: The Word of God is alive and present in this gathering.

A candle and a bowl of holy water serve as reminders of our baptism and our promise to follow Jesus. Have your children bless themselves with the water every time they enter. Keep the candle lit throughout the class, not just during prayer, to remind them of the light of Christ showing the way for the lesson. (If you teach young children, be careful when they are around a lit candle, and use your judgment as to its placement and how long it remains lit.)

Using Posters and Displays

Children are fascinated by images. Recall some of the statues and images in your childhood church. You can probably still picture some of them. One thing I (Gwen) remember from my childhood parish is that on special occasions four men—my dad was usually one of them—would carry what looked like a tent over to the priest who was carrying a monstrance (a large gold sun-shaped vessel in which the host is placed). The priest would walk under that "tent" all around the church, with an incense-bearing altar server walking backwards in front of him, bobbing the censer up and down. I loved this ceremony, and I especially loved the words written on the sides of the "tent": "At the name of Jesus, every knee should bend."

I know now that those men were carrying a *baldachin*, but whatever the name, that image of "reverence" instilled in me a deep sense of awe about the presence of Christ—in the eucharist and otherwise. Of course, many of the images I grew up with were very pious and sometimes sad, angry, or even scary. Still, they captured my attention and communicated something that words alone could not. Visual images possess great power.

Just so, the pictures, posters, and objects in your learning environment can convey a great deal to children: a sense of the sacred, wonder, joy, and reverence. These shouldn't be merely decorative. Think about what you want these things to "teach." Talk to your DRE about what's available. Have your class work together to create decorations, and display your students' work to enhance their self-esteem.

If you don't have a room you can call "yours," that does not mean you can't still introduce a visual touch. A standing display board is one way to do it. A three-panel display board, the kind kids use for science projects, can be purchased for just a few dollars at an office supply store. You can carry it with you to class, and place it in a prominent location during the lesson. When class is over, you can fold it up and take it home again.

Actually, use as many posters, pictures, and objects during your lessons as possible, ones that can be referred to or even passed around during the lesson.

Another Great Tool

A chalkboard is another great tool—one that you should use often and well. Once, when I (Joe) arrived to open the parish center for first communion class, I found the catechist impatiently waiting for me by the door—45 minutes early! When I let her in, she quickly dashed to her room and began writing and drawing all over the chalkboard.

She knew how to make the most of it. Writing out lists or questions beforehand, drawing pictures, or detailing instructions can save you class time and decrease the number of times you turn your back on the children, thus maintaining discipline. In addition, a chalkboard that is filled with ideas communicates to children that there is an organized plan here and that you are a competent facilitator.

If your catechetical setting does not have a chalkboard, you can use an overhead projector or an easel to engage your students visually. (Remember, children are going to retain only 20% of what they hear, but 50% of what they hear and see.) Be sure to make some notes on your lesson plan about when, where, and how you can best use the chalkboard, easel, or overhead projector to set the stage for your class and engage the children visually.

Small, But Important

There are a few more small things that are important for setting the stage. As part of your lesson planning, determine whether or not you're going to need anything copied to distribute, like a worksheet or an assignment that's not in your text. Be sure to arrange ahead of time to have copies made. Handing the children something as soon as they enter the room is one of the best ways of getting and keeping their attention.

Jesus didn't have to deal with electronics when he taught! But he did use storytelling and parables, the popular medium of his day. Our modern world is highly technological. But you don't have to be an electronics engineer to be a successful catechist. Just learning how to use video and audio recorders, and maybe even a computer, will enhance your ministry a great deal.

If you're showing a video, *always* preview it! If you are using a cassette tape, be sure you've looked over the equipment ahead of time. Few things can fluster a catechist as much as a piece of equipment that doesn't cooperate!

No class is complete without the necessary tools of the trade. Don't get caught reading directions that tell children to color a picture if you don't have crayons! Be sure to arrange with your DRE to have pens, pencils, crayons, scissors, index cards, and scrap paper on hand to help your little artists and writers express themselves. If children retain 90% of what they do, then it is crucial that you have the necessary tools to enable them to do their thing!

One more thing. God calls each of us by name. It's only right that we call the children we teach by theirs. Until you memorize their names, ask them to wear name tags or make name plates out of cardboard to place on their desks. When you interact with them, you can then honor them by calling them by name.

So far, we have covered some small but very important details that we think will really help you create the right environment for your religion class. Your DRE can probably provide you with access to all of the things we talked about: posters, prayer station materials, video cassette players, easels, pencils, crayons, etc.

But it's up to you to take the initiative to do some creative planning and brainstorming and then approach your DRE for access to these materials. Try hard to welcome the children into a setting that tells them, "This is going to be different from school." It takes a little more time and effort, but it's really worth it. Paying attention to all of these details is like looking over the road ahead to see if there are any potholes or detours in the way.

Catechesis from the Home

You might be thinking at this point, what about parishes that have religious instruction in the home, or what about parents who teach their children at home? How can they transform the setting so that it doesn't feel like it's time to sit in front of the TV?

Even when teaching at home, your goal is to welcome children into a community of shared faith, centered on the Word of God in Jesus Christ. While the home has a built-in inviting and welcoming atmosphere, a catechist still needs to communicate the special purpose of this gathering.

A prayer station should still be central to the gathering. While classroom desks and chairs are stiff, a living room sofa might be too casual. You will need to provide for a seating arrangement that will form community and enhance the catechetical process. One year, I (Gwen) taught a class in my home and after experimenting with various settings, I settled on the dining room. When children arrived they sat around the table (on which I had placed a Bible and a lit candle), and we began with a prayer service. After the prayer, I removed the Bible and candle and the table became an all-purpose space for reading, writing, drawing, and discussion. When I wanted to show a video, we moved into the room with the TV, but the dining room was my real teaching space.

Since most of us don't have chalkboards at home, and we're not likely to put posters on our walls, we can effectively use the kind of portable display board we described earlier for a visual focus. Some catechists use a write-on/wipe-off board that they can prop up on a chair or hold in front of themselves to write things down as they would on a chalkboard.

The bottom line is, teaching in the home does not take away the importance of preparing the environment for effective catechesis.

For Your Reflection and Discussion

• Recall some of the "places" where learning took place for you—which were the most effective learning environments and what made them so?

• Evaluate the space you are using this year. How conducive is it to faith development? What can be done to improve it?

• How can you make your teaching space more welcoming? What kind of seating arrangement works best for you and your class?

• Do you have a "prayer station" or "sacred space" set off as a visual reminder of the presence of God? How can you establish or improve such a space?

• What images and decorations are available to enhance your learning environment? Do you have all the materials you will need on a regular basis?

•Arrange to talk to your DRE or Coordinator to get ideas about making your teaching space more welcoming? Or talk to a veteran catechist who has a knack for creating a good learning environment.

A Catechist's Prayer

Holy Spirit, Spirit of the Risen Christ, I'm so concerned with getting lessons ready that I forget to think about how the children before me "feel." Help me to be aware of each of them, to reach out to them, and do my best to help them get comfortable in your presence. Open their minds and hearts to your Word in every class I teach. Amen.

In My Own Words...

_____

_____

_____

_____

_____

_____

_____

_____

_____

_____

Chapter Four

Ways to Motivate and Involve Children

Before you start reading, think about these questions: Do the children in your class seem happy to be there? Are they enthusiastic about your lessons and the activities you prepare? Do they participate in class discussions and reviews?

O ur work as catechists is a lot like taking a picture. To take a good one, we need the right equipment and the right setting. But ultimately, we need to engage our subjects in order to get what we're looking for. We need to motivate them to get just the right pose, the right look, the right smile. Good photographers interact with their subjects to get the desired results. But once the picture is taken, all they can do is stand back and wait to see how it develops. It's out of their hands.

As catechists, even with all the right equipment and all the right preparations, our success depends on our ability to motivate and involve our students. Once we've done all we can, we have to let go and trust that God will carry on the development of these children into the beautiful image of their full potential.

As we thought about this topic, we tried to recall teachers who have been successful in this area. The first person that I (Joe) thought of was Father John Powell, an author, speaker, and teacher who taught me in college. On the first day of class, he stood at the door and warmly greeted each of us forty students as we entered the room. Next, he produced a camera and arranged us in groups of six to eight for a snapshot. After taking the pictures, he had us put our names on the back in the order in which we appeared.

To our amazement, the next day, Father Powell greeted each of us by name. It seems he spent the night before studying the photos to match names with faces. Needless to say, he captured our attention and we were motivated to respond more fully to what he had to say.

So naturally, one of the first things I do when teaching a class is learn names and call children by their names. When we do this, we engage them at a *personal* level, calling forth their unique potential. This is not a gimmick or a technique. It's simply a way of recognizing and honoring the fact that each child in our class is created in the image of God, who calls all of us by name.

Interacting with Students

A teacher I (Gwen) will never forget moved around the room constantly and drew us into what she was teaching through body motions and voice expressions. She got my attention and held it. All of us can probably think of teachers who were engaging when they talked or interacted with us. We felt captivated by them, drawn in. They had a way of holding our attention. Jesus must have been such a teacher because the Bible tells us that his crowds were spellbound and amazed at how he taught with such authority. For some people this is a natural gift. For others, it takes work. Few of us will ever go on the circuit as a motivational speaker, but we can all learn some basic skills to engage our students by getting their attention and keeping it.

Overlooked Basic Skills

Let's be clear here. When we talk about engaging and motivating, we're not talking about entertaining our students. If we're entertaining them, that's nice, but as catechists we're not in show business. We're not talking about gimmicks or being flashy. We're talking about some basic skills that are quite frankly often overlooked in the catechetical ministry.

We've already talked about calling those we teach by name as they come into class. Let's backtrack a little and take a look at what needs to happen before you enter your teaching space. Most of us are familiar with the story of Ebenezer Scrooge. He was not an engaging person at all. He distanced himself from everyone in his life. Yet, in the end, he was transformed into a new person, engaging and outgoing. How did this transformation happen? Scrooge was changed because the three Spirits who visited him forced him to take an honest and painful look at himself: past, present, and future. This forced him to recognize some things about himself that needed change.

Taking a good honest look at ourselves can be very difficult. But, if we can see ourselves as we really are, we have a better opportunity to grow and improve as people. As a student teacher, many years ago, I had a very powerful experience of taking a good honest look at myself on video as I was teaching a class. Watching that video was in some ways very painful. However, at the same time, it had a very powerful and positive influence on me.

While I noticed many quirks and habits that I wanted to correct, I also found that I looked genuinely interested in what I was doing and communicated a great deal of enthusiasm. Recognizing my strengths and my weaknesses encouraged me to forge ahead and work to improve my teaching techniques.

Try the same process yourself. Videotape yourself teaching and when the class is over, sit down with a colleague or your DRE and view the video. I realize that we are very self-conscious about watching ourselves on tape, but like Ebenezer Scrooge, we stand a greater chance of improving ourselves if we take a good hard look at both our strengths and weaknesses.

What To Look For

If you do watch yourself on video, what should you look for? First notice how you move or don't move around the room. If you teach from your desk and never move around, it's very difficult to communicate enthusiasm. If you stand behind a podium, it looks like you want to be separated and distanced from your students. One of the best ways to hold attention is to move around. Move from your desk to the podium or to different parts of the class so that students are forced to keep contact with you visually. When you stand near children, they assume you are going to engage them personally and they pay better attention.

Something else you should look at is your eye movement. I (Gwen) had a teacher once who always looked at the wall behind us and never at us. It was disconcerting. It felt like he was talking to himself. We think it's important to look directly at those you teach. If you can learn to "ride your eyes" around the room, you can engage students' attention even when you are not the one speaking, and bring them closer to the center of activity.

A third thing to look for is what you sound like! Is your voice a monotone or are you communicating interest and enthusiasm? Listen to your pace and see if you're speeding ahead of children or losing them because you're too slow. Are you too loud or speaking too softly? Another thing to watch is your face. Are you communicating joy and enthusiasm, or do you look bored?

Obviously, all of us can stand to improve our ability to engage students by taking a good honest look at our teaching style and delivery. But let's move on now to some skills that will help us do this.

Get Attention Immediately

We have found that one of the best ways to engage students is to get their attention the minute they enter the room. As they enter, hand them a worksheet, an assignment, a puzzle, a picture to color, or an article to read. You will have thus succeeded in engaging them before they have had a chance to sit down. Certainly, you don't want to give them an overwhelming assignment that will turn them off. However, if you can hand out something as simple as an index card and ask them to write a list, a question, a comment, or some other information that will be pertinent to your lesson, you will be communicating the focus for the class right at the start.

Another effective way to get and keep attention is to ask good questions. Jesus regularly used questions to engage his audience: "Who do people say that I am?" "What is the inscription on this coin?" "What did you go out to the desert to see?" By using questions, he challenged individuals and whole groups of people to reflect on the deeper meaning of his teachings. Asking a question sounds so easy, but it requires some skill. And keep in mind that all questions are not equal. Some require a yes or no answer, for example: "Do you believe in God?" Some questions can be answered with only a word or two, for example: "Where was Jesus crucified?" Still other questions challenge children to bring what they personally believe into the answer. An example would be: "How does the crucifixion of Jesus affect your life? How do you feel about it?" It's important to use a variety of questions so that our lessons don't end up being lectures, but rather engaging and involving explanations of faith.

In addition to different types of questions, it's important to know how to ask them. Remember to phrase your questions in such a way as to avoid simple yes or no answers. If you are discussing the dangers of riches, for example, don't ask, "Would you like to be rich?" Instead, ask: "If you were rich, what would you do with your money?" This second question challenges children to express more fully their attitude toward money, sharing, greed, etc.

Answering Our Own Questions

Probably the biggest trap we catechists fall into is answering our own questions. We panic if we don't see a hand go up right away, so we simply answer the question ourselves. It's OK to give children time to think. If they still don't answer, try rephrasing the question, but don't answer it. Give them time to do that. It helps to move around the room slowly while children are pondering their answers, and to make eye contact with them. Then we can repeat the question to be sure they understand it.

It may seem like a lifetime, but nine times out of ten, someone will respond within seconds. If all else fails, you can call on someone who did not volunteer. When you ask a question, always ask it of the whole class first. If you call on one student and then ask a question, you've given an unconscious signal that the others don't have to pay attention to your question.

Finally, if one student answers, don't be satisfied. Always see if someone else has something to add before you move on. Your quiet students will often wait for that second invitation.

While on the subject of "answering," let me just add that it's OK if we don't know the answer to every question children ask. We are not doctrinal experts; we're Christian searchers. If we don't know the answer to a question, we can always say, "I don't know, but I'll find out for you by our next class."

Questions and answers often lead to further discussion, but unless a catechist is prepared, such discussions can lead to chaos instead of to learning. So how should you lead a discussion?

Guidelines for Discussion

First of all, always be sure you've introduced the topic well so your students will know what they are being invited to discuss. Second, be aware of your pace. Don't get bogged down on any one issue for too long, especially if the class is losing interest. Most important, don't get caught in a one-on-one exchange with a student while the rest of the class watches. Invite others to share what they think. Always be prepared to switch gears with a question that will keep the discussion relevant to your topic.

Third, practice giving feedback to your students. Praise and reward play a big part in motivating and building self-esteem. Children participate more if they feel you are interested in what they have to offer. Be sure to tell them, "That's excellent" or "That's a very good point you've made." Also be prepared to respond to wrong answers without embarrassing anyone. Instead of saying, "No, you're wrong," you can say something like, "Nice try, and let's see if someone can add anything."

Finally, it's important that you bring your discussions to a clear conclusion. Nothing is more frustrating than the feeling of being left hanging. A good discussion should be summarized by you or by a student and wrapped up with a clear statement of what was accomplished and where you are headed.

Remember, too, discussion is not an end in itself. It is a tool through which we hope to teach something about our faith. Discussion has its place, especially in the first stage of catechesis where we explore the life experiences of children. It's difficult to explore these without some type of sharing. Discussion plays a big role, too, in the last stage of catechesis, where we try to integrate the content of our tradition with the life experience of the children.

There are many creative activities that can engage and motivate students, and they all have their place. We believe that asking questions and leading pertinent discussions are two of the most effective ways. They can help you to gauge whether children are grasping the content of your lessons and whether they are applying what they learn to their daily life and decisions. Isn't this after all one of our primary goals as catechists?

For Your Reflection and Discussion

•Can you recall a teacher who motivated you particularly well? What makes this teacher stand out for you?

•How do you feel when someone calls you by name? What can you do to remember your students' names?

•Have you ever seen yourself "in action" on video? How did you assess your performance? If you've never been taped, can you arrange for someone to videotape you and then discuss the tape with you?

•Do you move around the room when you teach? Are you comfortable doing so? How is your eye contact? How do you feel when someone talks to you but doesn't look at you?

•How patient are you when waiting for an answer to a question? Do you try to use a variety of questions? Which type works best for you?

•Do you ever allow children to enter into discussion? What discussion techniques have worked best for you?

A Catechist's Prayer

Jesus, Son of God and Blessed Companion, if I am to motivate those I teach, I need you to motivate me. Help me to remember that it is your Word I proclaim, your presence I point to. Motivate me, please, to be the best religion teacher I can be. Amen.

In My Own Words...

Chapter Five

Handling Discipline Problems

Before you start reading, think about these questions: Is maintaining control of a group of children difficult for you? What are your worst problems? Would you enjoy teaching more if you could develop discipline skills? Is there someone in your program who could guide you?

As catechists, we are dedicated to bringing the Word of God to children through a variety of creative approaches. We want to invite them into a deeper relationship with Jesus Christ in every class we teach. Sounds easy, right? It would be if our listeners were all well-behaved, attentive, and fully interested in our lessons.

It would also be easier if we always prepared our lessons as carefully as possible. Sometimes, however, in spite of our best efforts, we fail to get and keep attention. We are convinced that with the proper skills and techniques we can at least minimize many of the discipline problems we face. That's what we'll be looking at closely in this chapter.

When I (Joe) was teaching high school, I periodically had a dream—actually a nightmare. In this dream, I would enter my classroom only to find thirty unruly students who were screaming and yelling and throwing things. The more I tried to get their attention, the weaker my voice got until in a panic I would try yelling to get their attention, but no sound would come out.

It turns out that many catechists and teachers share this frustrating dream. One of our greatest fears is losing control of our students. Discipline problems are to be expected when we work with children and teenagers. However, we *can* minimize and even prevent some of them. If we are well equipped with the proper skills and techniques, we can often defuse potential problems before they take form.

The Root of the Problem

But before we talk about skills and techniques, let's take a closer look at the problem of discipline, which is a lot like the common cold. If we are constantly showing symptoms of a cold—coughing, congestion, stuffy nose, and so on—we are probably not eating right, getting enough rest, or exercising properly. We can treat cold symptoms with medications, or we can get to the root of the problem.

The same is true of discipline. If our classes are continually showing symptoms of poor discipline, we can either treat the symptoms, or we can get to the root of the problem. The truth is, most discipline problems are the result of poor teaching techniques. In fact, if you are doing all the things we talked about in our previous four chapters, you will minimize and even prevent most of your discipline problems.

It's also true, though, that even those of us in the best of shape will occasionally catch a cold. Even the best teachers will still occasionally encounter discipline problems. Good discipline, however, is not our goal. Sound catechesis is.

Maintaining discipline is like removing obstacles in the path toward our goal. We need to learn how to remove and avoid these obstacles so that our destination can be reached.

Typical Discipline Problems

Let's begin by taking a look at a few "typical" discipline problems that every catechist faces. We have organized them into three categories: minor, moderate, and major.

In the minor category, we have *wavering attention*. As we all know, children's attention spans can be very short. Second is *distractions*. Many children are easily distracted by the most insignificant things. Third is *side talking*. This is when two or three children begin talking among themselves when they should be listening or participating as a class.

Under moderate discipline problems, we have *the child who separates him or herself* from the rest of the class and refuses to be a part of the whole. Second is *simple mischief*. Children will often engage in behaviors that end up disrupting the entire class, throwing spitballs, for example. Third is *talking out of turn*. While most children learn to raise their hands, some will continually shout out answers or questions out of turn, thus disrupting the order of the class.

Finally, here are the major discipline problems. The first is *chaos*. Sometimes, when a project or activity is underway, the group as a whole loses focus and chaos results. Pushing and shoving are an example of this. Second is what we call *sabotage*. This is the problem of one or more students planning ahead of time to ruin or obstruct the lesson (by tampering with equipment, for example). Third is *disrespect* or *dishonesty*. At times children will act out behaviors that are seriously opposed to gospel values, like stealing or lying.

These examples are not meant to frighten you, but only to

alert you to some possible situations that may arise. All of them can be dealt with in a professional and effective manner with the proper skills and techniques. When it comes to such discipline problems, we definitely should not panic! The minute we feel control slipping away, our tendency is to lose our cool. An effective catechist knows how to respond firmly but calmly. If we lose control, the children may lose respect for us and, even worse, may find our outbursts entertaining—and so continue to test our limits.

It's also good to try to deal with discipline problems without interrupting our lesson. Discipline antics are ways of seeking attention. If we can give children the needed attention through eye contact, calling on them, walking near them, or placing a hand on shoulders to let them know we want them to pay attention, we can keep the lesson flowing. The worst thing is to repeatedly stop to correct someone. No one benefits except the child who wants attention.

Noticing Everything

In her book, *Discipline Made Easy* (Twenty-Third Publications), Sr. Kathleen Glavich has a chapter called "Noticing Absolutely Everything." In some ways, as her book suggests, teachers do need to have eyes in the back of their heads. In reality, this means that we have to be keenly aware of many things at once. It's not easy, but it comes with experience. Let's look at some DOs and DON'Ts that will enable you to be more in control of some of the minor discipline problems we have mentioned here.

DO learn to ride your eyes. We may not have eyes in the back of our heads, but we have to use the eyes we have as effectively as possible. By riding your eyes around the room, you can engage students without saying a word.

DO call upon students using their names. If a student's attention is wavering, it helps to call on him or her to answer a question which invites the child back into the circle of activity. Remember, using names really helps.

DO move around the room. If children are side talking or distracted, you can bring them back into the action by walking near them and placing a hand on their shoulder. This will allow you to keep the lesson going without interruption.

DO check your seating arrangement. Some children just need space. Alter your seating arrangement to separate children who distract one another so that they can concentrate better on the lesson.

DO assign tasks and responsibilities. Most children are looking for attention. If you can assign tasks such as distributing and collecting materials, you can successfully and constructively engage those who lose interest quickly.

DO use nonverbal communication. As much as possible, try to engage students without interrupting your lesson. Nonverbal communication such as waving your hand, shaking your head, or just a facial expression can send a clear message.

DO reinforce good behavior. We all know the famous saying, accentuate the positive. Well, that applies to discipline as well. If we concentrate on rewarding good behavior, we will provide children with the positive attention they are seeking and we will be minimizing their need to act out.

DON'T turn your back or leave the room. If you need to have things written on the board, try to do so ahead of time so you can point to them instead of turning your back. And never, never leave the room unattended.

DON'T continually stop your lesson. If children see that they can stop the lesson and derail you by small disruptions, they will do so. Show the children that you can handle more than one thing at a time by keeping your lesson going while you tend to a minor discipline problem.

DON'T allow problems to escalate. Discipline problems can start small and snowball. Be sure to promptly give attention to problems before they get out of hand. Don't ignore them. They won't go away.

These techniques can go a long way toward minimizing minor discipline problems, but it also helps to have a healthy dose of patience. Don't let the little things get to you. When you deal with minor problems patiently, they aren't as apt to overwhelm you.

Moderate Discipline Problems

Obviously, not all problems can be handled this simply. "Moderate" problems call for the addition of class rules that should be established by teacher and children and referred to often. You might even invite children to help enforce them. In addition to class rules, let's also look at some DOs and DON'Ts for handling discipline in this moderate category.

DO keep a sense of humor and perspective. If you keep things in perspective, you will find that many of these problems can be reduced to minor ones. With the proper sense of humor, you may be able to totally defuse a situation.

DO be firm, confident, and consistent. When problems surface, you need to take a deep breath, be sure you have the behavior in perspective, and then deal with it firmly and with confidence. You need to be in control of the situation. Above all, you need to be consistent. If you come down on a certain behavior for one child, you need to do it for all.

DO post and enforce your class rules. Too many rules can communicate the wrong message, so keep it simple. Many catechists consider the following three rules essential: No interrupting others (including the teacher); No putting others down; No yelling, pushing, or running. Again, you will want to establish your own basic rules, post them, and abide by them.

DO show respect and understanding. When children misbehave, we can become very irritated. It's important to deal with discipline situations calmly and show respect for the children. Remember, it is to ones like these that the kingdom of God belongs.

DO confront and identify the behavior. As soon as a problem occurs, confront and identify it. In other words, without verbally attacking the child, address the inappropriate behavior.

DON'T use sarcasm or criticize publicly. Let's be honest. We catechists *can* lose our cool. In such situations, it is imperative that we not use sarcasm to put kids down or embarrass them in front of their peers. We need to use appropriate language when addressing our students. Deal with problems after class whenever possible to avoid public situations.

DON'T use homework as a punishment and don't make God a law enforcer. Such strategies only backfire. We want children to have a positive image of assignments, and certainly we want to teach about God as one who loves them unconditionally, not as one who punishes.

DON'T force involvement. Some children have a good reason for not participating. Always invite; never force a child to do something he or she does not want to do.

Dealing with Major Problems

Problems like chaos, sabotage of equipment, and dishonesty and disrespect certainly belong in the "major" category. Let's look at the DOs and DON'Ts for these.

DO prepare, organize, and provide clear expectations. Chaos in the classroom can occur at any time, especially when a project or activity is under way. Before you engage your class in out-of-the-ordinary projects, be sure you are well prepared. Have your plan and materials well organized. Above all, communicate the plan with precise expectations.

DO be fair and flexible and negotiate a contract. When dealing with serious problems, it is important to deal fairly with children. Be sure you have informed them of the consequences of certain behaviors ahead of time. By negotiating a contract with individual students, you allow room for forgiveness and the possibility of improvement.

DO consult parents, your DRE, or colleagues. Don't try to solve serious problems alone. Seek the advice of your peers, especially those who are veterans. Above all, make sure you communicate with parents about serious matters and ask them to assist you in dealing with inappropriate behavior.

DON'T punish the whole class for the offense of one. At times, out of frustration, we may feel that we have no other recourse, but it is simply unfair to punish the whole class because of something one student has done.

DON'T accuse or verbally attack a student. Even though we may be extremely upset in a situation, it is imperative that we never accuse a child of something or unleash a verbal assault. Calmly state your feelings by saying, "I am upset that this has happened," rather than, "You did this or that." When speaking with parents, do not accuse their children, but rather ask if they are aware of similar behaviors.

DON'T begin class until you have attention. If you are undertaking a class activity or project, don't begin until you are sure you have everyone's attention and all understand exactly what is expected of them.

DON'T ever, ever leave your class unattended. This cannot be stressed enough. Acts of dishonesty, disrespect, or sabotage will most likely occur when the teacher is not around. If you are present and on top of the situation, such behaviors are unlikely to occur.

Two Essential Ingredients

We haven't mentioned the two essential ingredients of prayer and love. As catechists, we need to pray for guidance when handling serious matters. And in our prayer we need to ask the Holy Spirit to help us respond to children with love, no matter how frustrated we feel. Even when you do feel overwhelmed, don't give up. Trust that God will guide you in the person of your DRE and other teachers in your program.

Again to quote Sr. Kathleen Glavich (who quotes Dick Van Dyke): "A teacher must have the faith of Abraham, the patience of Job, the wisdom of Solomon, the courage of Daniel as he goes into the lion's den, and the confidence of Moses that it is all worthwhile." I can't emphasize this point enough. Jesus faced some pretty tough audiences, and so have prophets and preachers down through the ages. The work of a prophet is never easy. As catechists, we are called to be prophets for those we teach. Let us pray often for the strength and determination to persevere in this very special task.

For Your Reflection and Discussion

•With what kinds of discipline problems are you most familiar? What kinds of discipline problems did you cause when you were a child?

•Recall one of your teachers who had good discipline without being an "ogre." What did that person do successfully to keep discipline in class?

•What is your biggest discipline "nightmare"? What can you do to minimize the possibility of such a problem?

•What are some ways you can handle discipline without interrupting the flow of your lessons?

•Who are the catechists in your parish who handle discipline problems effectively? What do they do well that you are not doing? How can you learn from them?

•What class rules do you consider most essential?

A Catechist's Prayer

Jesus, my Brother and Friend, you know all about my discipline woes. Help me to learn creative ways to deal with difficulties and to be positive in my relationships with every child I teach, no matter how hard that sometimes is. Speak through me, teach through me, and discipline through me. Amen.

In My Own Words...

_____

_____

_____

Chapter Six

Helping Children to Pray

Before you start reading, think about these questions: Why should prayer be a priority for catechists? Do you allow time for prayer in every class you teach? How much time should you allow? Do you use a variety of prayer forms?

The *National Catechetical Directory* tells us that "all catechesis is oriented to prayer and worship." Prayer is at the very heart of the Christian life and our catechetical ministry. Catechists have the awesome responsibility of inviting children to deepen their relationship with Jesus through prayer. Leading meaningful prayer experiences is a skill that can be learned and developed.

I'm sure most of us were taught as children that prayer is "talking to God." While that's a good start, it's a rather incomplete definition of prayer, and consequently most of our prayer is words: talk, talk, talk. If this is your experience of prayer, your class prayer experiences might be compared to making a cake that has only one ingredient. A typical cake has five or six ingredients, and, even after it's baked, we can make it even tastier and fancier by adding frosting and decorations. We can make eating the cake a celebration by playing music or decorating the room. But if the cake has only one ingredient, nobody will want to eat it.

St. Paul told the Christians in Ephesus to pray always. So, surely he wasn't referring to prayer as words only. As catechists we need to know that good prayer, as with a good cake, has many ingredients. Words are important, but we also need silence, music, symbols, ritual, movement, gesture, and last but certainly not least, listening.

All of these are the ingredients that together make up the cake we call "prayer." We need to approach prayer as something we do with our whole self, not just with words. If we can get beyond prayer as talking to God and teach our children to approach prayer as being in touch with and being touched by God, we will be helping them to "pray always."

We Are Not Experts

While class prayer may sound difficult, keep in mind that we don't have to be spiritual gurus to lead children in meaningful prayer experiences. Leading prayer experiences involves the same qualities that are needed for effective teaching. We have to prepare well, with clear goals for the prayer experience. We need to prepare the prayer environment and prayer materials, and to focus on ways to involve the children so that it's not just us talking. We need to examine our own leadership style to see how we can best communicate prayerfulness and reverence, and we need to be prepared to handle behavior and discipline problems effectively without interrupting the flow of the prayer.

So a catechist who possesses good teaching skills and also has a good understanding of prayer should be able to lead children in class prayer experiences. But prayer experiences have a unique dimension in that they involve a sacred time. We need to carefully choose the right moment. Before and after class can sometimes be the worst time because children are either not settled in yet or are ready to go home. Prayer should always be at the "heart" of the lesson.

It's also important, as we have already noted, to have an area set aside as "sacred space," a place where children know that something different happens. This kind of space is really important. Even though God is always with us, we need to make sacred space to "tune in" to this presence.

Children Need Quiet

Just like us, children need time to quiet themselves and become aware of God's presence. It's not easy for them to be quiet for too long. But all of us need some quiet space in our lives. We all need solitude. We do our children a great service if we allow them space for solitude, a space out of which they can focus and quiet themselves, and out of which they can talk to and listen to God. This can be done by inviting the children to practice some breathing exercises, or by playing peaceful background music that fades into silence. Either way, the transition from activity to silence should be gradual.

Let's get back to our cake image for a moment. There are many different types of cakes we can bake for a variety of occasions: pound cake, angel food cake, pineapple upside-down cake, birthday cakes, wedding cakes, and so on. Well, the same is true of prayer. Prayer can be expressed in a variety of ways for a variety of occasions. The important thing is knowing what the occasion is for prayer, and what ingredients can best be used to make that prayer take shape. Let's take a look at some of these prayer ingredients and see what skills a catechist needs to utilize them.

All prayer is a response to God. All of our class prayer experiences should give children the opportunity to respond to God's action in their lives. And there are a variety of ways for them to respond. Some are nonverbal and some are verbal. Most of us include verbal responses like traditional prayers, Scripture verses, and singing.

Nonverbal elements are often overlooked, but they are very important. One nonverbal element is silence. A good prayer leader knows how and when to use moments of silence during the prayer experience to allow children to get in touch with the presence of God. Good prayer also includes signs and symbols, such as holy water, candles, incense, and banners. Combined with silence, such objects can be powerful symbols of God's presence in children's lives.

Other nonverbal elements are movement and gesture. If we are to pray with our whole bodies, we need to be comfortable moving about in prayer. Movement and gesture can involve such things as processions, the passing of a candle, the lighting and placing of a candle, placement of objects or pictures in the center of the prayer space, or even something as simple as standing in a circle with arms interlocked. Movement and gesture can include more dramatic elements such as liturgical dance and ritual movement of our bodies. This takes a great deal more preparation and requires sensitivity to the children's readiness for such expression.

Writing or drawing can also be elements of prayer. It's probably more accurate to call these non-oral forms of prayer, because, while words are involved, children aren't speaking them out loud. Another important ingredient in class prayer is posture. Let children try a variety of postures, such as sitting on the floor, standing, and participating in ritual movement.

Although singing has an element of words to it, it's not the same as the spoken word. Music and singing are important ingredients that allow children to express themselves, while at the same time allowing the Word of God to speak to them.

Whichever of these techniques you use, remember that class prayer should be communal prayer. Encourage children to pray privately, of course, but during class, always invite group participation. Children in religion class are a community of believers who are experiencing together the presence of the risen Christ.

What About Formal Prayers?

Though we haven't mentioned them specifically, what about formal prayers? Is there still a place for teaching children traditional prayers and using them in our prayer experiences? Absolutely! We have a great tradition of formal prayer: the Our Father, the Hail Mary, the Glory Be, the Act of Contrition, the Morning Offering, and many others. Formal prayers are part of our faith heritage.

By teaching them to children, we pass on this heritage. Because children know the words by heart, they can pray these prayers together as a faith community. So yes, formal prayers should often be a part of our class prayer experiences because they are a part of who we are as a Christian community. We need to be careful, however, not to rely solely on traditional prayers so that we don't fall into the trap of letting prayer become just "talk, talk, talk."

The following is an actual prayer experience that includes a variety of ingredients: silence, music, symbols, involvement, and motion. For it, you will need a tape player, background music on tape, drawings or pictures of animals (one for each child in your class), a Bible open to Genesis 8:15–19 and 9:12–17, and copies of the readings for the five readers.

Catechist: Boys and girls, we have been learning about Noah's Ark and how God's promise to Noah is a sign of hope. Let's spend time in prayer now thanking God for the signs of love and hope in our lives. Close your eyes for a minute and get quiet. As you do so, picture yourself with Noah coming out of the ark and seeing the rainbow up in the sky.

(As children sit quietly play soft background music.)

Catechist: Open your eyes now and look at the pictures I will give you. One by one, I'd like each of you to stand up and show your picture to the rest of the class. (Appoint one child to begin.) Let's listen now to Noah's story in the Bible.

Reader One: Then God said to Noah: "Go out of the ark, together with your wife and your sons and your sons' wives. Bring out with you every living thing that is with you—all bodily creatures, be they birds or animals or creeping things of the earth—let them abound on the earth, breeding and multiplying on it."

Reader Two: So Noah came out, together with his wife and sons and his sons' wives; and all the animals, wild and tame, all the birds, and all the creeping creatures of the earth left the ark, one kind after another....

Reader Three: God added: "This is the sign that I am giving for all ages to come, of the covenant between me and you and every living creature with you: I set my bow in the clouds to serve as a sign of the covenant between me and the earth.

Reader Four: "When I bring clouds over the earth, and

the bow appears in the clouds, I will recall the covenant I have made between me and you and all living things, so that the waters shall never again become a flood to destroy all mortal beings.

Reader Five: "As the bow appears in the clouds, I will see it and recall the everlasting covenant that I have established between myself and all living beings—all mortal creatures that are on earth." God told Noah: "This is the sign of the covenant I have established."

Catechist: Whenever we see a rainbow, it can be a sign of hope for us. All of us hope for things. Think for a moment about some of the things you hope for. As I again play some music, look at your animal picture. When you know what it is you are hoping for, quietly tell God about it. Then, when you've finished praying to God, get up and place your picture on our prayer table as a sign that all of your hopes will be in God's hands.

(After all the pictures are on the table, continue as below.)

Catechist: God promises to take care of us and knows what our hopes are. We have just shared some of them with God. Let's end our prayer now by thanking God for the gift of hope. Let's stand and join hands. After each of the prayers I will say, please respond, "Thank you, God, Amen."

Catechist: Thank you, God, for all the animals you have created...

All: Thank you, God, Amen.

Catechist: Thank you, God, for blue skies, for rain, and for rainbows...

All: Thank you, God, Amen.

Catechist: Thank you, God, for being with us and talking to us in prayer...

All: Thank you, God, Amen.

Catechist: Thank you, God, for giving us hope...

All: Thank you, God, Amen.

Services like this one need not be elaborate, but they should include silence, movement, verbal prayer, meditation, prayer objects, and rituals. If possible, involve children in the planning. Let them draw the animals, read the Scripture, and carry the Bible and (unlit) candle to the prayer table.

Prayer is one of the best ways to remember the presence of Jesus, to remember that he is always with us. And it is an essential ingredient in every class we teach. We conclude with this message from Jesus to his followers—and to us:

"Go, therefore, and make disciples of all nations, baptizing them in the name of the Father, and of the Son, and of the Holy Spirit. Teach them to carry out everything I have commanded you. And know that I am with you always until the end of the world."

For Your Reflection and Discussion

•When you pray with your class, what do you usually do? Do you use "words" primarily? In what ways do you pray without words?

•Recall a meaningful prayer experience you have had with your class. What made this prayer experience effective?

•Do you have a designated prayer space in your teaching area? Why or why not? How often do you use it?

•How do you make the transition from your lesson into prayer? How do you prepare children for communicating with God?

•What nonverbal elements do you use in your class

prayer experiences? Do you ever use ritual gestures, movement, silence, guided meditations? How have these worked for you?

•How often do you use formal, traditional prayers with your class? Are there ways that you can combine these with other forms of prayer?

A Catechist's Prayer

Jesus, my Teacher and Savior, I have been helped so much by your presence in my life. I want to share with those I teach all the many ways they can talk to you, walk with you, and rest in you. Enlighten me and guide me that I may truly be a person of prayer and a teacher of prayer. Amen.

In My Own Words...

_____

_____

_____

_____

_____

_____

_____

_____

Chapter Seven

Evaluating Yourself

Before you start reading, think about these questions: Why is it important to look closely at your teaching skills and techniques? How might you improve after such a close look? Who can help you to be honest and thorough in your evaluation?

So far we have covered some very important teaching topics: qualities, skills, and techniques of a good catechist; planning lessons; creating a positive faith environment; motivating children; maintaining discipline; and ways to plan meaningful prayer experiences. It is only fitting then that we look back at these topics as part of an overall evaluation process.

Qualities and Techniques

As you look at each of the qualities below, rate yourself good (G), fair (F), or poor (P).

Don't be discouraged if you aren't able to mark "good" on all of them. Let your fair and poor items challenge you to do better in every class you teach.

____Am I committed to the practice of my faith and to my ministry as a catechist?

____Am I enthusiastic about helping children to grow in their faith?

____Am I flexible enough to adapt my lesson plans when necessary?

____Do I always study my teacher's manual before preparing my lessons, and do I consult other available resources?

____Am I patient with those children who find it hard to pay attention?

____Do I always arrive on time, well before the children?

____Do I try to have a sense of humor when things go wrong?

____Do I make the most of the teaching space I am using and of the materials that are available to me?

____Do I handle discipline problems with compassion and understanding?

____Am I prayerful, and do I frequently offer children opportunities to pray?

____Do I take the time needed to prepare my lessons well, and do I always keep the needs of the children in mind?

Planning Good Lessons

Since some of the questions above concern lesson planning, in this category you might want to focus more on the variety of methods you use to teach your lessons. For example, look at the list that follows and answer yes (Y) if you use the method regularly and no (N) if you rarely, if ever, use it.

____reading from the text

____watching videos

____playing games (using material from your lessons)

____leading group discussions

____role-playing, plays, or skits

____craft projects

____writing and drawing

____journaling

____sharing time for prayer

____using music, singing, and dancing

The point of using a variety of methods is to keep children actively involved in learning about their faith. If you always read from the text or always lecture, children probably lose interest quickly. If you use methods that aren't listed here, all the better. If they work well, share them with other catechists at your next gathering.

A Positive Faith Environment

Even catechists who must use a small or otherwise undesirable space for their teaching are probably able to do something to make it better. What about you? How do you make your existing space better? How do you make it more welcoming? How do you seat children, and how does your seating arrangement work for you?

Do you have a prayer space in your teaching area and how do you decorate it? Do you use signs, handouts, and posters? Is there something you would do differently if you could? What will you do differently for your next class?

Motivating Those You Teach

One of the primary ways a good teacher or catechist motivates children is by being present to them. When they know they are important in the eyes of the teacher, children are far more apt to pay attention and do well. So, how are you doing at motivating? Rate yourself below as good (G) or not so good (N).

_____Am I enthusiastic about what I am teaching?

_____Do I move around the room a lot?

_____Do I keep eye contact at least some of the time with every child in my class?

_____Am I loud enough, clear on my directions, and organized?

_____Do I keep children busy with a variety of activities?

_____Do I challenge children with my questions, and do I use a variety of questioning techniques?

_____Am I consistently fair?

Handling Discipline Problems

This is the hardest area for many catechists. Yet, many discipline problems can be averted with good lesson plans. But perhaps you do plan well and still have problems. How do you handle them? How often do you use the following techniques? Answer with always (A), sometimes (S), or never (N).

_____Do you have clear class rules and do you stick to them? Do the children understand your rules?

_____Do your eyes ride the room on a regular basis and do you move around frequently?

_____Do you call on all students (without favoritism) to answer questions, and do you call them by name?

_____Do you reinforce good behavior through praise, and do you encourage cooperative learning rather than competition?

_____Are you firm, confident, and consistent in your response to unacceptable behavior?

_____Do you show respect and understanding for every child?

_____Do you confront and identify unacceptable behavior right at the outset?

_____Do you keep a good sense of humor?

_____Do you consult your DRE or colleagues about problems you can't handle alone, and do you talk to parents when necessary?

Leading Prayer Experiences

As I hope we have made abundantly clear, prayer should be an essential element of every religion class. It could be argued that prayer is the goal of all that we teach. A person of prayer is in touch with God and if we have guided children toward a relationship with God, we have done a great deal indeed. So, how are your prayer experiences? What works best for you, and how can you tell? What do children respond best to? Do you use a variety of prayer experiences (including the following)? Answer yes (Y) or no (N).

_____Is there a special prayer space in your teaching area?

_____Do you always allow time for silent prayer?

_____Do you sometimes use music and singing?

_____Do you use rituals like blessings, holding up objects, holding hands, sharing a sign of peace?

_____Do you sometimes allow children to write their own prayers?

_____Do you encourage them to plan class prayer services?

_____Do you pray for every child in your class on a daily basis?

Don't be discouraged if you answer no to several items. Again, use the results of your evaluation to motivate yourself to do better next time.

Keep in mind that one of the easiest ways to pass any evaluation with flying colors is to plan ahead. Having said that, here's a checklist you might want to use in late summer or in the fall as you prepare for a new group of children. Look closely at any unchecked items and do whatever it takes to be prepared—before your classes begin.

A Final Checklist

____Do I know exactly where I will teach and am I familiar with the physical setting?

____Do I know how many children will be in my group, and do I have a list of their names?

____Do I have access to parents' names and phone numbers?

____Do I know whether it will be my responsibility to contact parents about disciplinary problems or program goals?

____Have I resolved to arrive at least ten minutes before the children?

____Do I know where I can get audiovisuals and other materials such as paper, pencils, crayons, and glue?

____Have I made a list of creative activities I could use through the year?

____Have I considered the importance of music (song and dance) for religious education?

____Have I thought about incorporating prayer in each lesson?

____Have I developed a possible strategy for handling discipline problems when they arise?

____Do I know someone who can assist me from time to time with special projects and field trips?

____Do I have the name and phone number of a possible substitute in case I cannot teach on a certain day?

____Have I discussed my fears, insecurities, misunderstandings with my DRE?

____Have I talked with, prayed with, other catechists?

____Have I sought advice from experienced catechists in my parish program?

____Have I read the introductory and supplementary material in my teacher's manual?

____Am I familiar with the student text?

____Have I read any reference material, books, articles that are available?

____Will I have access to a religious education magazine, perhaps my own subscription to *Religion Teacher's Journal*?

____Have I resolved to reflect upon the material I will be teaching at least a few minutes each day?

____Do I try to be a person of prayer, in touch with God who has called me to my teaching ministry?

Why Should You Bother?

The question naturally arises: Why bother to evaluate yourself as a catechist? The more pressing question, however, is, why not? You certainly want to help children enter into a relationship of love with God, and by improving your skills, habits, and techniques as a catechist you will be able to do this even better.

As already noted, evaluation is certainly not intended to discourage you, but rather to motivate you to be the best catechist you can be. During the process, focus on what you do well and resolve to improve on those things that need improvement. Above all, evaluate yourself with love—as God always evaluates you.

One final note: Try to find time in your busy schedule to reflect on this passage from the prologue of the *Catechism of the Catholic Church*. It sums up and beautifully describes our role as catechists.

"The whole concern of doctrine and its teaching must be directed to the love that never ends. Whether something is proposed for belief, for hope or for action, the love of our Lord must always be made accessible, so that anyone can see that all the works of perfect Christian virtue spring from love and have no other objective than to arrive at love."

For Your Reflection and Discussion

If you have completed the questions in this chapter, you are no doubt all-questioned-out. So for a change of pace, complete the following phrases, either alone or with a group of catechists. Answer spontaneously rather than studiously. Often what we really think or feel is the first thing that comes to mind when asked.

I think I have grown as a catechist, especially in the areas of...

_____

_____

I would say my greatest strength as a catechist is...

_____

_____

My greatest weakness as a catechist is...

_____

_____

One thing I have learned from the children in my class is...

_____

_____

I feel that Jesus (God, the Holy Spirit) is guiding me when...

_____

_____

If I could do one thing over again during this teaching year, it would be...

_____

_____

One thing about being a catechist I will never forget is...

_____

_____

A Catechist's Prayer

Jesus, Blessed Savior, it is so difficult to look at my teaching with a critical eye. I would rather not face my weaknesses and I certainly don't want others to evaluate me. Yet, you have chosen me and you love me, weaknesses and all. Help me to grow and blossom and to be open to the suggestions of others. May those I teach blossom and grow as well. I place them in your care this day and always. Amen.

In My Own Words...

_____

_____

_____

_____

_____

_____

_____

_____

_____

_____

For Catechist Enrichment

All of the following resources are available from Twenty-Third Publications, P.O. Box 180 (185 Willow St), Mystic, CT 06355. Phone: 1–800–321–0411; Fax: 1-800-572–0788; E-mail: ttpubs@aol.com.

Video Programs

Empowering the Catechist
Skills and Techniques for Effective Teaching
Joseph Paprocki
This video series is based on the content of this book. Topics include the importance of catechetical ministry, lesson planning, a positive environment, motivating students, discipline, and prayer. Especially convenient to use in parishes where professional training is not available. Comes with a leader's guide and a free copy of *Creative Catechist*. Six 30-minute sessions, $99.00.

Enriching the Catechist
Brennan Hill and William Madges
This six-part video program will help catechists add richness and theological continuity to their religious education programs. Two well-known theologians and a diverse team of religious educators identify and discuss fundamental doctrines of the Catholic faith and issues of theological importance. Appropriate for teachers of all grade levels. Six 30-minute sessions, $99.00.

Magazine

Religion Teacher's Journal
This catechetical magazine, published seven times annually during the school year, focuses on religion teachers and their spiritual, pedagogical, and practical concerns. It offers regular columns on discipline, theology, spirituality, lesson planning, saints, youth ministry, catechetical resources, games and activities, and much more.

Resource Books

Creative Catechist: A Comprehensive, Illustrated Guide for Training Religion Teachers
Janaan Manternach and Carl Pfeifer
This is an ideal book both for in-service and pre-service teacher training. Catechists will find practical help here with lesson planning, discipline, classroom techniques, student motivation and grading, use of media to enrich lessons, guides to class prayer—all the elements that enable a religion teacher to become a creative catechist. $12.95.

Prayer Services for Catechist and Teacher Meetings
Gwen Costello
These 30 services offer participants an opportunity to pray together and grow in the habit of prayer. Each is a complete prayer experience that also teaches valuable faith lessons and can be used for meetings during the school year and specifically for the beginning of a new teaching year, All Saints, Thanksgiving, Advent, Christmas, Lent, Easter, Pentecost, and Ordinary Time. $12.95.

Tools for Teaching: Classroom Tips for Catechists
Joseph Paprocki
This do-it-yourself manual offers step-by-step instructions for approaching a wide variety of catechetical challenges: planning lessons, handling discipline problems, using textbooks and teacher manuals, praying with your class, and choosing appropriate activities. A great companion for new catechists and a real refresher course for veterans. $7.95.

Discipline Made Easy: Positive Tips and Techniques for Religion Teachers
Mary Kathleen Glavich, SND
This informative and practical book offers hundreds of tested techniques to provide encouragement to new volunteer catechists and wise insight to veterans. An excellent guide for religion teachers at any grade level. $7.95.

Leading Students into Scripture
Mary Kathleen Glavich, SND
Here Sr. Kathleen offers hundreds of suggestions for involving children in Scripture—through prayer, games, activities, crafts, interviews, plays, and much more. $12.95.

Jesus, I'm a Teacher Too
Guidance and Inspiration from the Gospels
Melannie Svoboda, SND
Whether used for personal or group reflection and prayer, this book will help religion teachers learn from St. Mark's Jesus what it means to be a dedicated teacher. The author reveals the compassion and gifts of Jesus, the master teacher. Insights and inspiration abound. $9.95.

*Teaching Is Like...*Peeling Back Eggshells
Melannie Svoboda, SND
The author suggests that a teacher is like a farmer helping young chicks to hatch by gently peeling back a portion of the eggshell so as to ease the birth (of new ideas for students). Warm and witty, these fifty reflections of an outstanding teacher will give catechists the boost they need to continue the important task of being effective, enthusiastic teachers. $7.95.

A Way of the Cross for Religion Teachers
Gwen Costello
At each stop on Jesus' way to Calvary, catechists are given insights into the challenges and trials of their ministry through this unique devotional booklet. It's ideal for teacher meetings during Lent and also for personal prayer. $1.95.

A Teacher's Prayerbook
To Know and Love Your Students
Ginger Farry
Written by a full-time teacher who often brings her students to God, this delightful book contains prayer poems for and about students. These prayers chronicle the good and bad days, the joys and

disappointments in the life of a teacher. Each prayer is followed by a brief reflection or questions for teachers to ponder in relation to their own students. $4.95.

Five Dynamic Dimensions for Effective Teaching
Kevin Treston
This contemporary book describes five important aspects of a teacher's vocation: integrity, wisdom, generativity, learning, and justice. The author encourages teachers to foster these qualities so as to be learning companions with students on the journey of life and faith. $9.95.

A Prayer Primer for Catechists and Teachers
Gwen Costello
Here catechists and teachers are offered personal advice about how to develop a habit of prayer and ways to share prayer with those they teach. Topics covered include personal prayer, praying with children, praying with the Bible, and using rituals for prayer. Also included are prayers to accompany religion teachers through the year. $5.95.

Models and Trends in Religious Education
Gail Thomas McKenna
An experienced DRE offers other DREs and Coordinators insights and information about the many ways parishes can now offer religious education: family style, lectionary based, parish clusters, total youth ministry, and through the RCIA process. $19.95.

God's Word Is Alive!
Entering the Sunday Readings
Alice Camille
Here DREs, catechists, and teachers will find commentaries for all three cycles of the Sunday readings. The commentaries are contemporary, clear, and refreshing. Each offers new insights about the readings. Questions for discussion are included. $19.95.